SIGNS OF THE TIMES

TEXT AND PHOTOGRAPHS BY • TEXT UND PHOTOS VON

• TEXTE ET PHOTOS DE: KLAUS F. SCHMIDT

EDITED BY • REDAKTION • RÉDACTION: B. MARTIN PEDERSEN

PUBLISHER AND CREATIVE DIRECTOR: B. MARTIN PEDERSEN

BOOK PUBLISHER: CHRISTOPHER T. REGGIO

EDITOR: CLARE HAYDEN

ASSOCIATE EDITOR: PEGGY CHAPMAN

PRODUCTION DIRECTOR: VALERIE MYERS

ART DIRECTOR: JENNIFER THORPE

GERMAN EDITOR: BARBARA JÜRGENSEN PALMER

GERMAN TRANSLATION BY: ASTRID VON CHAMIER

FRENCH TRANSLATION BY: KIRSTEN KEPPEL

LIBRARY OF CONGRESS CATALOG CARD NUMBER: 96-76149, ISBN 1-888000-11-9, © COPYRIGHT UNDER UNIVERSAL COPYRIGHT CONVENTION, COPYRIGHT © 1996 BY GRAPHIS U.S., INC., FRONT COVER PHOTO BY LUDOVIC MOULIN/ GRAPHISTOCK, INC. ALL OTHER PHOTOGRAPHS COPYRIGHT © 1996 BY KLAUS F. SCHMIDT, JACKET AND BOOK DESIGN COPYRIGHT © 1996 BY PEDERSEN DESIGN, 141 LEXINGTON AVENUE, NEW YORK, N.Y. 10016 USA, NO PART OF THIS BOOK MAY BE REPRODUCED IN ANY FORM WITHOUT WRITTEN PER-MISSION OF THE PUBLISHER, PRINTED IN SINGAPORE BY CS GRAPHICS PTE LTD.

GRAPHIS U.S., INC.

TOP ENTERTAINMENT

FLOOR SHOW

DELICIOUS FOOD BRING THE FAMILY

TOLL GATE

HISTORICAL SHOW PLACE OF THE OLD WEST

BUFFALO BILL DRANK Here

A WILD SWINGIN' CRAZY JAMBOREE

SINCE 1876 The WORLD FAMOU

TO

VAUDEVILLE

Contents • Inhaltsverzeichnis • Sommaire

(Preceding spread) **Central City**, Colorado 1969; (Opposite) Petrified Forest, Arizona 1972; (Page 6) South Street, New York 1970; (Page 16) Plymouth, England 1985; (Page 50) San Francisco, California 1967; (Page 70) Geneva, Switzerland 1976; (Page 102) Killarney, Ireland 1994; (Page 142) Cusco, Indiana 1980; (Page 160) Bermuda, 1966; (Back Cover) London, England 1969

INTRODUCTION

EINLEITUNG

INTRODUCTION

M. RUMELY CO.
RUMELY
LAPORTE
PLOWING
HULLING AND THRESHING
LAPORTE IND.

igns of the Times is a collection of signs whose graphic, typographic and painterly designs have caught my eye during years of travel around the world. My interest in the typography and graphics of the streets reaches back to my training as a printer, compositor and typographic designer in Germany after World War II. Over the years I have traveled extensively and always with my 35mm camera. Initially I used an Agfa Karat 36, then a Leica M4 and M5, and in later years a Canon A-1. I frequently annoyed my travel companions when I insisted on lying flat on the ground or on climbing ladders, fire escapes and rock outcroppings to train my lens on some fascinating bit of street or highway graphics. Over the years, my slide collection has grown to formidable proportions, so selecting the images for this book, my first, was not easy. These pictures are of more than visual objects—they evoke memories of precious moments past, and of fascinating, faraway places. The signs found in this collection range from tavern shields to traffic symbols, from store shingles to political and advertising banners. Extending the subject of signs to include all "graphics under the skies," this collection also contains gravestones, mailboxes and clock surfaces which bear lettering.
■ The first known commercial sign was that of a dream analyst in ancient Egypt around 300 B.C. Streets in Rome and Greece were filled with signs indicating inns and taverns, as well as professional and trade establishments. In Europe during the Middle Ages and the Renaissance, signs for "public houses" and craft shops became increasingly ubiquitous. Many were executed in elaborate, wrought-iron styles. Others were painted on wooden boards, frequently in simple, readily understandable pictorial designs, since literacy was not widespread. Signs were traditionally manufactured by resident village or city painters who had rarely been exposed to formal printing or compositional training. If they contained lettering, they were usually uninhibited with regard to the correctness of period type styles and

letterforms. Fortunately, a good number of painted signs, especially in the British Isles and in Northern and Central Europe, have survived. Though they have often been extensively retouched, repainted or reconstructed, their folk art quality of simplicity and cosy old-worldliness intrigue today's observers. ■ Today, signs are made of a wide variety of media, from wood, stone and wrought iron to glass, sheet metal and neon tubing. We are drawn to the texture of peeling paint on seasoned wood and the fading and torn poster collages on European Litfass kiosks and walls. Weathered walls with fading, nostalgic messages formed in muted color patterns or "canvases" of brownish brick rectangles are prevalent in American towns. Such early commercial display typefaces are often emulated in our own times. One also encounters the typographic romanticism of the arts-and-crafts movement or the modernity of Art Nouveau or Art Deco. ■ Our eyes are also intrigued by signs we can not decipher. Passages from the Koran in Arabic script on the walls of mosques and Islamic palaces and the strange shapes of American Indian petroglyphs on the sandstone rocks of Arizona's Petrified Forest appeal to our sense of mystery and design. ■ Rusted, weathered highway signs once warned motorists in their dust coats, goggles and leather caps of an impending curve. In modern times, traffic signs in the United States have generally included more written language than in multilingual Europe, where motorists are accustomed to the symbolism of standard traffic signs. This has resulted in an abundance of pictographs in Europe and other parts of the world which Americans have been slow to adopt. ■ Contemporary directional signs frequently utilize well-known sans serif (and more rarely serif) typefaces. Because of the speed of today's vehicular and pedestrian traffic, the letterforms have often been modified and the letter spacing opened up to increase legibility at a distance. ■ In today's commercial world, signs appear in ever–increasing varieties. Some may be described as impressive and exquisitely conceived. Others are commonplace and primitive. Many are downright ugly and environmentally disturbing. In comparison with Europe, America's streets and highways are garish, predominantly due to an overabundance of signs. Adrian Frutiger, the renowned Swiss type designer, aptly describes this excess of signs as "pictorial noise." Nevertheless, signs do express the spirit of an era and establish time and place for the viewer. In our mobile age, they must be visually grasped in split–seconds and are often overpoweringly eye-catching. ∎ All those who walk or drive through the streets with open "typographic eyes," as well as those who peruse these pages will be treated to a multitude of eye-pleasing graphic and typographic designs found on signs. KLAUS F. SCHMIDT, NORTH TARRYTOWN, NEW YORK, MAY 1996

. . . .

Signs of the Times ist eine Sammlung von Schildern und Inschriften, deren graphisches, typographisches und malerisches Design mir während meiner jahrelangen Reisen um die Welt ins Auge gefallen ist. Mein Interesse an der Typographie und Graphik der Straßen reicht zurück bis in meine Ausbildungszeit als Drucker, Setzer und typographischer Designer in Deutschland nach dem Zweiten Weltkrieg. Im Lauf der Jahre bin ich — immer mit meiner 35mm-Kamera — weit gereist. Anfänglich benutzte ich eine Agfa Karat 36, dann eine Leica M4 und M5, und in späteren Jahren arbeitete ich mit einer Canon A-1. Häufig verärgerte ich meine Mitreisenden, wenn ich darauf bestand, flach auf dem Boden zu liegen oder auf Feuerleitern und Felsvorsprünge zu klettern, nur um meine Kamera auf ein faszinierendes Objekt der Straßentypographie zu richten. Im Lauf der Jahre hat meine Dia-Sammlung beachtlichen Umfang angenommen, so daß die Auswahl für dieses Buch, mein erstes, nicht leicht war. Diese Bilder sind mehr als nur Objekte zum Anschauen — sie rufen Erinnerungen hervor an kostbare Momente der Vergangenheit und bezaubernde Orte in weiter Ferne. Die in dieser Sammlung vorgestellten Objekte reichen von Kneipenschildern bis zu Verkehrssymbolen, von Ladenschildern bis zu Wahl- und Werbeplakaten. Die Begriffe "Schilder und Inschriften" umfassen im weiteren Sinne alle "Graphiken unter freiem Himmel". So enthält diese Sammlung auch Grabsteine, Briefkästen und Ziffernblätter von Uhren, die beschriftet sind. ∎ Das erste uns bekannte Geschäftsschild war das eines Traumdeuters im alten Ägypten um 300 v. Christi. Die Straßen in Rom und Griechenland waren übersät mit Schildern, die hinwiesen auf Gasthäuser und Schenken wie auch auf Handels- und Handwerkshäuser. In Europa wurden während des Mittelalters und der Renaissance Hinweisschilder auf Gasthäuser und Läden allgegenwärtig. Viele waren in sorgfältig geformtem Schmiedeeisen ausgeführt. Andere waren auf Holzbretter gemalt; in der Regel in einfachen, leicht verständlichen Bildsymbolen, da die Lesefertigkeit noch nicht weit verbreitet war. Herkömmlicherweise wurden Schilder von ortsansässigen Malern angefertigt, die selten im Drucker- oder Setzerhandwerk ausgebildet waren. Enthielten die Schilder Schrift, so waren sie gewöhnlich recht frei den korrekten zeitgenössischen typographischen Stil- und Buchstabenformen nachempfunden. Glücklicherweise hat eine ganze Anzahl gemalter Schilder überlebt, insbesondere auf den britischen Inseln und in Nord- und Mitteleuropa. Obwohl sie oft umfassend retuschiert, übermalt oder rekonstruiert worden sind, fesselt die Einfachheit dieser Volkskunst und ihr an die Gemütlichkeit der Alten Welt erinnernder Stil noch heute den Betrachter. ■ Heutzutage sind Schilder aus einer Vielzahl von Materialien gefertigt — von Holz, Stein und Schmiedeeisen bis hin zu Glas, Blech und Neonröhren. Wir fühlen uns angezogen von der Struktur abblätternder Farbe auf verwittertem Holz und den ausbleichenden, zerrissenen Kollagen auf europäischen Litfaßsäulen. In amerikanischen Städten finden sich häufig verwitterte Hauswände, "Leinwände" aus braunem Ziegel, mit verblassenden, nostalgischen Botschaften und Mustern in gedämpfter Farbe. Man findet Schrifttypen der Werbung aus dem 19. Jahrhundert, die heute oft nachgeahmt werden. Oder man erkennt den typographischen Romantizismus der Arts-and-Crafts-Bewegung oder die Modernität von Jugendstil oder Art Deco. ■ Unsere Augen bleiben auch hängen an Inschriften, die wir nicht entziffern können. Passagen aus dem Koran in arabischer Schrift auf den Wänden von Moscheen und islamischen Palästen und die fremdartigen Formen indianischer Felszeichnungen auf den Sandsteinfelsen im Versteinerten Forst Arizonas sprechen unseren Sinn sowohl für Geheimnis als auch Design an. ■ Rostige, verwitterte Verkehrsschildern warnten einst Autofahrer in Staubmänteln, Schutzbrillen und Lederkappen vor einer kommenden Kurve. In den USA wird heute auf Verkehrsschilder im allgemeinen mehr Schrift verwendet als im vielsprachigen Europa, wo die Verkehrsteilnehmer an die Symbolik standardisierter Zeichen gewöhnt sind. Dies führte in Europa und anderen Teilen der Welt zu einem Repertoire von Piktogrammen, an das sich die Amerikaner nur langsam angepaßt haben. Zeitgenössische Wegweiser benutzen häufig die gebräuchlichen Groteskschriften und seltener das Antiqua-Schriftbild. Aufgrund der Geschwindigkeit des heutigen Auto- und Fußgängerverkehrs wurden die Buchstabenformen oft modifiziert; die Buchstabenabstände wurden erweitert, damit die Schilder aus der Entfernung besser lesbar sind. ■ In der gegenwärtigen Geschäftswelt werden Schilder in wachsender Vielfalt verwendet. Manche sind ein-prägsam und schön entworfen, andere wiederum sind ordinär und primitiv. Viele sind geradezu häßlich und verunstalten die Umgebung. Im Vergleich mit Europa sind Amerikas Straßen auffällig und grell, vor allem weil sie mit Schildern überladen sind. Adrian Frutiger, der bekannte Schweizer Schriftdesigner, beschreibt dieses Übermaß an Zeichen und Schildern als "Bild-Lärm". Nichtsdestotrotz spiegeln Schilder den Geist einer Ära wieder und etablieren Raum und Zeit für den Betrachter. In unserem mobilen Zeitalter müssen sie in Sekundenschnelle erfaßbar sein, und sie springen oft geradezu ins Auge. Alle, die mit offenen "typographischen Augen" durch die Straßen gehen oder fahren, wie auch jene, die diese Seiten sorgfältig durchblättern, werden Freude finden an einer Vielzahl von gefälligem graphischen und typographischen Schilderdesign.

KLAUS F. SCHMIDT, NORTH TARRYTOWN, NEW YORK, MAI 1996

. . . .

Signs of the Times est une collection d'enseignes et de panneaux dont les designs graphique, et typographiques ont attiré mon atten-tion pendant des années où j'ai voyagé partout dans le monde. Mon intérêt dans la typographie et le graphisme des rues a commencé dès ma formation d'imprimeur, de compositeur et de typographe en Allemagne après la deuxième guerre mondiale. Au cours des années, j'ai beaucoup voyagé, toujours avec mon appareil-photographique de 35mm. J'ai commencé par utiliser un Agfa Karat 36, puis un Leica M4 et M5, et plus récemment, un Canon A-1. J'ai souvent agacé mes compagnons de route en insistant à m'allonger par terre ou à grimper les échelles, les escaliers de secours, et les affleurements de rochers afin de fixer l'objectif de mon appareil sur une partie fascinante des graphiques visibles dans des rues ou le long des autoroutes. Au fil des années, ma collection de diapositives a atteint des proportions impressionnantes. Sélectionner des images pour cet ouvrage, qui constitue mon premier livre, n'était pas facile. Ces images sont beaucoup plus que les reproductions d'objects physiques — ils évoquent les souvenirs des moments précieux passés et des endroits lointains. On trouve dans cette collection des enseignes allant de celles d'auberges jusqu'aux symboles de circulation; des enseignes des boutiques jusqu'aux bannières politiques et publicitaires. Si on permet au sujet d'inclure tous les "graphiques sous les cieux", cette collection est alors dotée d'autres perspectives bien importantes: on peut y faire figurer les pierres tombales, les boîtes à lettres et les surfaces des horloges à gravures. ■ La première enseigne commerciale connue était celle d'un analyste de rêves en Egypte, 300 ans avant Jésus Christ. A Rome et en Grèce, les rues débordaient d'enseignes d'auberges et de cabarets, d'établissements professionnels et commerciaux. Au Moyen-Age et à l'époque de la Renaissance, les enseignes en Europe des "maisons publiques" et des maisons artisanales sont devenues de plus en plus omniprésentes. Beaucoup d'enseignes étaient réalisées dans un style élaboré en fer forgé. D'autres étaient peintes sur les planches en bois, apparaissant souvent comme des dessins pictoraux facilement compréhensibles, l'alphabétisme n'étant toujours pas très répandu. Les enseignes étaient traditionnellement fabriquées par les peintres du quartier. Il était très rare que ceux-ci connaissent les techniques de l'impression formelle ou de la formation compositionnelle. Si une gravure quelconque y figurait, elle y apparaissait sans égard pour l'exactitude des styles typographiques de l'époque. Heureusement que plusieurs enseignes peintes aient survécu, surtout dans les îles britanniques, en Europe centrale, et en Europe du Nord. Bien qu'elles aient été considérablement retouchées, repeintes ou reconstruites, leurs qualités de simplicité et d'intimité émanant de l'art populaire du Vieux Monde, intriguent l'observateur d'aujourd'hui. ■ A notre époque, les enseignes sont fabriquées à partir d'une grande variété de matériaux : du bois, de la pierre et du fer forgé jusqu'au verre, au métal et aux tuyaux au néon. Nous sommes inclinés à graviter vers les textures de peinture qui pèlent sur le bois seché et sur les collages d'affiches fâdes et déchirées aux murs et dans les kiosques du Litfass européen. Les murs exposés aux intempéries, portant des messages nostalgiques en motifs de couleurs sourdes, soit les "toiles" de rectangles brunâtres en brique, sont partout dans des villes américaines. De tels caractères commerciaux sont souvent imités à notre époque. On trouve aussi le romantisme typographique de l'artisanat ou la modernité de l'Art Nouveau, ou de l'Art Deco. ■ Les enseignes indéchiffrables éveillent aussi notre curiosité. Les passages du Coran apparaissant dans un script arabe sur les murs des mosquées et des palais islamiques, et les étranges pétroglyphes des indiens américains apparaissant sur le grès des rochers dans la "Forêt pétrifiée" d'Arizona, font appel à notre sens du mystère et du design. ■ Les signes routiers rouillés, exposés aux intempéries, avaient autrefois fonctionnés comme les panneaux avertisseurs pour les motoristes vêtus en jaquette, lunettes, et casquette en cuir. A notre époque, les panneaux de signalisation aux Etats-Unis ont généralement plus de langage écrit que ceux d'une Europe multilingue, où les automobilistes sont habitués au symbolisme figurant sur les panneaux. En conséquence, en Europe et dans d'autres parties du monde, il existe une répertoire de pictogrammes que les Américains, eux, ont été lents à adopter. Les panneaux indiquant une direction utilisent très souvent les caractères sans-sérif (et plus rarement, sérif). A cause de la vitesse de la circulation véhiculaire et piétonne, la taille des caractères a souvent été modifiée et leur espacement a été changé pour qu'ils soient plus lisibles. ■ Dans le monde commercial contemporain, les enseignes sont d'une variété de plus en plus croissante. On peut dire que certaines sont impressionnants et conçues avec beaucoup de finesse, alors que d'autres sont communes et même primitives. Beaucoup sont franchement laides et dérangent l'environnement. Les signes routiers américains sont criards comparés à ceux que on trouve en Europe. Ceci est dû à la surabondance de panneaux qu'on trouve sur les routes américaines. D'après le concepteur suisse Adrian Frutiger, il s'agit d'un "bruit pictural". Pourtant, les panneaux et les enseignes expriment l'esprit d'une époque et oriente l'observateur vers un temps et un espace. A l'heure où la mobilité prime, il faut pouvoir comprendre les panneaux en un rien de temps. Ils captent souvent le regard de façon irrésistible. Tous ceux qui se promènent dans les rues ou qui conduisent avec leurs "yeux typographiques" ouverts, ainsi que ceux qui lisent attentivement ces pages, jouiront d'une multitude de designs graphiques et typographiqes esthétiques.

KLAUS F. SCHMIDT, NORTH TARRYTOWN, NEW YORK, MAI 1996

Until the end of the 1700's, commercial signage in North America followed predominantly British traditions featuring restraint in typography and graphics rooted in folk art. By the early 1800's traditional typographic usage had given way to excessively ornamented, drop-shadowed, fat and slab-serifed display types. Incongruous mixtures of letterforms flourished. Some of the graphic styles of the nineteenth century and a preponderance of fonts have carried over to our times. The design of signs in Britain and Ireland has also been influenced by the decorative display typefaces of that era. ■ While in North America such lettered signage reaches back just three centuries, European and Arab signs and formal inscriptions encompass millennia and thus exemplify much wider typographic styles. After the Roman alphabet, Arabic script is the second most widely used today. To those Western eyes which don't understand Arabic script, signs and inscriptions in the Arabic world appear mysterious and fascinating on a visual, graphic level. ■ Bis zum Ende des 18. Jahrhunderts folgte die Geschäftsbeschilderung in Nordamerika vor allem britischen Traditionen, deren Hauptcharakteristika die Zurückhaltung der Typographie und die in Volkskunst wurzelnde Graphik waren. Im frühen 19. Jahrhundert aber wurde die überlieferte Einfachheit aufgegeben zugunsten üppig geschmückter, fetter Schrifttypen, oft mit Schlagschatten und Egyptienneserifen. Uneinheitliche Zusammensetzungen von Schrifttypen standen hoch im Kurs. Die graphischen Stilarten des 19. Jahrhunderts und eine Vielzahl von Schriften gibt es teilweise heute noch. In Großbritannien und Irland ist das Schilderdesign ebenfalls vom dekorativen Plakatschriftstil dieser Zeit beeinflußt worden. ■ Während solche Beschriftungen in Nordamerika nur höchstens drei Jahrhunderte zurückreichen, umfaßt die Tradition europäischer und arabischer Inschriften Jahrtausende und weist daher eine viel größere Bandbreite typographischer Stilarten auf. Nach dem lateinischen Alphabet ist die arabische Schrift die heutzutage meist benutzte Schrift. Allerdings mögen arabische Zeichen und Schilder westlichen Augen, die die arabische Schrift nicht verstehen, in visueller und graphischer Hinsicht geheimnisvoll und faszinierend erscheinen. ■ Jusqu'à la fin des années 1700, les panneaux commerciaux en Amérique du Nord étaient construits pour la plupart selon des modèles britanniques. Ces panneaux étaient caractérisés par une certaine restreinte typograhique et des graphiques émanant de l'art populaire. Au début des années 1800, l'usage traditionnel typographique avait cédé la place aux caractères trop ornés, trop ombrés, trop gros et en sérif rectangulaire. Des mélanges incongrus de typographies ont fleuri. Certains styles graphiques du 19è siècle, ainsi qu'une prépondérance de polices, ont survécu jusqu'à nos jours. Le design des panneaux en Grande Bretagne et en Irlande a été également influencé par les caractères décoratifs de cette époque. ■ En Amérique du Nord, les caractères utilisés sur les panneaux existent depuis trois siècles, tandis qu'en Europe et dans le monde arabe, les panneaux aux inscriptions formelles datent depuis des millenia et illustrent des styles typographiques bien plus variés. Après l'alphabet romain, le script arabe est l'alphabet le plus utilisé aujourd'hui. Aux yeux des Occidentaux qui ne comprennent pas l'arabe, les panneaux et les inscriptions du monde arabe paraissent mystérieux et fascinants aux niveaux graphique et visuel.

Circus Wagon at Circus World Museum, Baraboo, Wisconsin 1974 • Zirkuswagen im Circus World Museum, Baraboo, Wisconsin 1974 • Chariot de cirque au Musée du Cirque, Baraboo, Wisconsin 1974

Sturgis, South Dakota 1989

Wall, South Dakota 1989

Bartlett, New Hampshire 1966

Dawson Creek, British Columbia, Canada 1993

Jackson, New Hampshire 1971

Atlanta, Georgia 1978

French Lick, Indiana 1992

Fort Nelson, British Columbia, Canada 1993

Fort Nelson, British Columbia, Canada 1993

Wall, South Dakota 1989

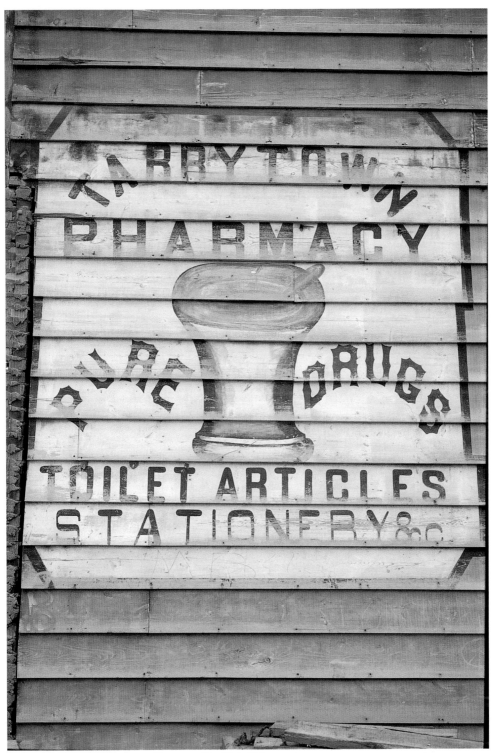

◄ **Jackson,** New Hampshire 1966 ▲ **Tarrytown,** New York 1970

Indian Lake, New York 1963

Old Quincy Market, Boston, Massachusetts 1969

Yellowstone National Park, Wyoming 1976

Jim Thorpe, Pennsylvania 1988

Chicago, Illinois, 1994

Nantucket, Massachusetts, 1973

Whistler, British Columbia, Canada 1993

Golden, Colorado 1984

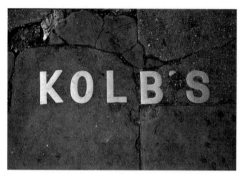

Pavement sign for a restaurant • Restaurantschild im Bürgersteig • Enseigne de restaurant, New Orleans, Louisiana 1972

Seafood Wholesaler, South Street, New York, New York, Fulton Fish Market, 1971

Fort Nelson, British Columbia, Canada 1993

St. Charles Hotel, New Orleans, Louisiana 1972

Tombstone, Arizona 1973

Bethlehem, Pennsylvania 1991

Jackson, New Hampshire 1974

Old Quincy Market, Boston, Massachusetts 1969

Steamtown USA, Bellows Falls, Vermont 1970

South Newfane, Vermont 1974

San Francisco, California 1985

Jackson, New Hampshire 1966

Marion, Ohio 1974

St. Joseph, Missouri 1994

Tarrytown, New York 1991

Hudson, New York 1992

San Francisco, California, 1985

Old Quincy Market, Boston, Massachusetts 1968

Old Quincy Market, Boston, Massachusetts 1968

San Juan, Puerto Rico 1988

San Juan, Puerto Rico 1988

Moroccan Railway logo, Marrakech, Morroco 1972 • **Logo der marokkanischen Eisenbahn,** Marrakech, Marokko 1972
• **Le logo des chemins de fer marocains,** Marrakech, Maroc 1972

▲**Mosque,** Istanbul, Turkey 1979 ▶**Asni,** Morocco 1972

GASOIL

مجموع الثمن

0 5 6 4

مجموع الليتروات

0 7 5 20 15

ثمن الليترو

 4 7 5

SATAM
La Courneuve - Seine

Marrakech, Morocco 1972

▲ **Mobil Gas Station,** Rabat, Morocco 1972 • **Mobil-Tankstelle,** Rabat, Marokko 1972 • **Station d'essence Mobil à Rabat,** Maroc 1972 ▶ **Fes,** Morocco 1972

Inverness, Scotland 1985

Carnaby Street shop, London, England 1969 • **Laden in der Carnaby Street,** London, England 1969 • **Boutique à Carnaby Street,** Londres, Angleterre 1969

◀▲ **Printing company,** Bristol, England 1985 • **Druckereifirma,** Bristol, England 1985 • **Imprimerie à Bristol,** Angleterre 1985

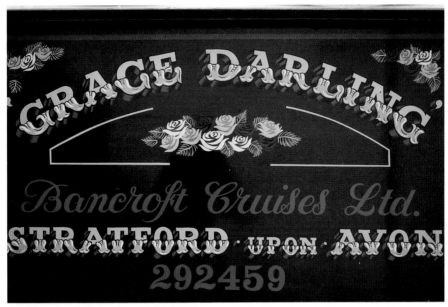

Canal boat, Stratford upon Avon, England 1985

Whitehall, London, England 1965

Chiswick, London, England 1985

Paris, France 1963

Paris, France 1969

Farm house, Watenstedt near Braunschweig, Germany 1990 • **Bauernhaus,** Watenstedt bei Braunschweig, Deutschland 1990 • **Maison de ferme à Watenstedt,** près de Braunschweig, Allemagne 1990

Erfurt, Germany 1992

Husum, Germany 1990

City Hall, Cochem, Germany 1972 • **Rathaus,** Cochem, Deutschland 1972 • L'hôtel de ville de Cochem, Allemange 1972

Street sign, Berlin, Germany 1992 • **Straßenschild,** Berlin, Deutschland 1992 • **Enseigne des rue, Berlin,** Allemagne 1992

Store in Nördlingen, Germany 1970 • **Geschäft in Nördlingen,** Deutschland, 1970 • **Boutique à Nördlingen,** Allemagne 1970

Berlin, Germany 1987

Rüdesheim, Germany 1980

Weimar, Germany 1992

Quedlinburg, Germany 1987

utomobiles, trains and ships have all exhibited an enchanting variety of visual graphics and typographic messages. Names of ships have traditionally been lovingly lettered in fanciful type styles on their bows or sterns, particularly during the nineteenth century on American paddle wheelers that plied the Mississippi, the Ohio, the Sacramento and the Hudson rivers. Railroads have been copiously equipped with signals, signs and symbols. Decades after the passing of steam power in regular service, the symbol of a steam engine is still employed as a traffic warning sign in some European countries. ■ Sowohl Autos, Züge wie auch Schiffe weisen eine erfreuliche Vielfalt in Graphik und Typographie auf. Schiffsnamen sind traditionellerweise liebevoll in ornamentalen Schriften am Bug oder Heck angebracht, insbesondere während des 19. Jahrhunderts auf amerikanischen Schaufelraddampfern, die den Mississippi, den Ohio, den Sacramento und den Hudson befuhren. Eisenbahnstrecken sind stets reichlich mit Signalen, Zeichen und Symbolen ausgestattet worden. Und noch Jahrzehnte nachdem die Dampfkraft aus dem regulären Betrieb verschwand, findet sich das Symbol der Dampflokomotive auf manchen europäischen Verkehrsschildern. ■ Les voitures, les trains et les navires ont tous fait preuve d'une variété fascinante de graphismes visuels et de messages typographiques. Les noms des navires ont traditionnellement été tendrement gravés sur la proue ou sur la poupe dans des styles typographiques pleins d'imagination, surtout pendant le dix-neuvième siècle quand les bâteaux à roues américains ont navigué sur les fleuves Mississippi, Ohio, Sacramento et Hudson. Les chemins de fer ont été copieusement équipés de panneaux de signalisation et de symboles. Plusieurs décennies après la fin des locomotives à vapeur, le symbole de celle-ci est toujours utilisé comme un panneau avertisseur dans certains pays européens.

Cripple Creek, Colorado 1973

Roanoke, Virginia 1981

Rensselaer, New York 1981

Nyack, New York 1968

Mystic Seaport, Connecticut 1970

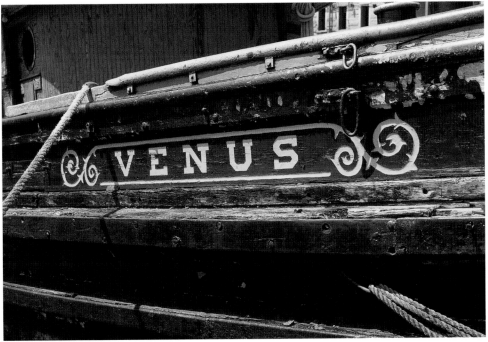

Boston, Massachusetts 1983

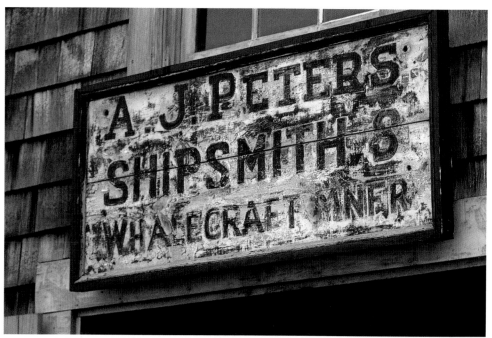

Mystic Seaport, Connecticut 1970

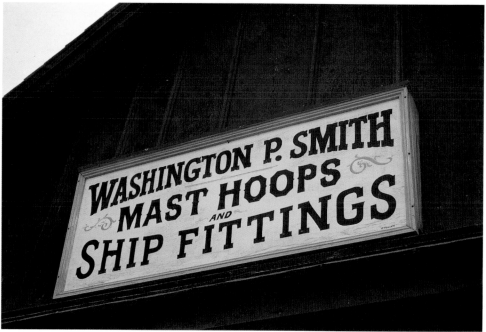

Mystic Seaport, Connecticut 1970

Newport, Rhode Island 1982

Mystic Seaport, Connecticut 1970

New Haven Railroad Car, Providence, Rhode Island 1971 • **Wagen der New Haven Railroad,** Providence, Rhode Island 1971 • **Un autorail de la ligne New Haven,** Providence, Rhode Island 1971

Martisco, New York 1976

Alexisbad, Germany 1977

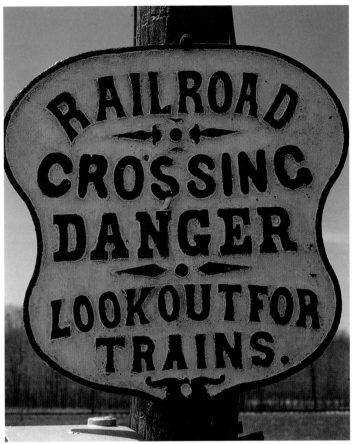

Wheaton, Maryland 1974

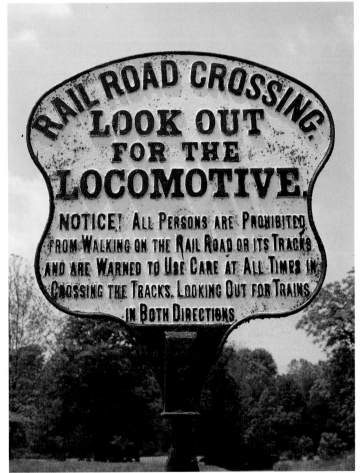

Kempton, Pennsylvania 1987

▲ **Berlin,** Germany 1987 ▶ **Copenhagen,** Denmark 1990

IKKE TIL REKOMMANDEREDE BREVE
IKKE TIL BREVE INDEHOLDENDE PENGE

POSTBREVKASSE

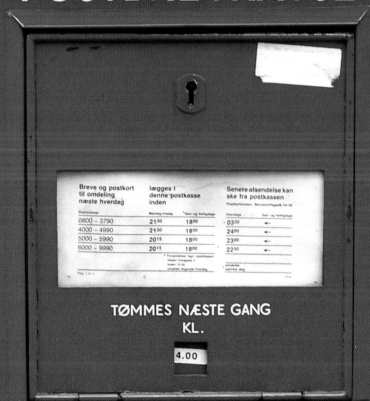

Breve og postkort til omdeling næste hverdag	lægges i denne postkasse inden		Senere afsendelse kan ske fra postkassen	
Postnumre	Mandag–fredag	*Søn- og helligdage	Hverdage	Søn- og helligdage
0800 – 3790	21³⁰	18⁰⁰	03³⁰	←
4000 – 4990	21³⁰	18⁰⁰	24⁰⁰	←
5000 – 5990	20¹⁵	18⁰⁰	23⁰⁰	←
6000 – 9990	20¹⁵	18⁰⁰	22³⁰	←

TØMMES NÆSTE GANG
KL.

4.00

Oviatt Building, Los Angeles, California 1979

Marrakech, Morocco 1975

Hamilton, Bermuda 1974

Bremen, Germany 1979

Cochem, Germany 1972

U.S.
MAIL
RURAL
ROUTE
Delivery
No. 1

◄ Mail delivery wagon, Jackson, New Hampshire 1971 • Postwagen, Jackson, New Hampshire 1971 • Wagon-poste à Jackson, New Hampshire 1971 ▲ Hoosick, New York 1971

Casablanca, Morocco 1972

Lucerne, Switzerland 1983

VILLE DE GENÈVE

✳

MUSÉE
ARIANA

✳

CÉRAMIQUE

ACADÉMIE INTERNATIONALE
DE LA CÉRAMIQUE

✳

ENTRÉE LIBRE

H. Loutan & fils

SIGNS OF THE STREETS
SCHILDER DER STRASSEN
ENSEIGNES DES RUES

Signs denoting places of business are more prevalent than ever. Such signs range from primitive, naive and amateurish to well-proportioned, sophisticated and irresistibly exciting. The most readily recognized of such signs display the logos and trademarks of international corporations seeking to extend their commercial influence. Street signs, while also ubiquitous, communicate information which has a more immediate impact on our lives, such as the rules of the road or the distance to our destination. ■ *Firmenschilder sind auffälliger denn je. Solche Beschilderung reicht vom Primitiven, Naiven und Amateurhaften bis zum Wohlproportionierten, Hochentwickelten und unwiderstehlich Anziehenden. Am leichtesten zu erkennen sind Schilder mit Logos und Warenzeichen internationaler Firmen, die ständig ihren wirtschaftlichen Einfluß zu vergrößern suchen. Verkehrsschilder sind auch allgegenwärtig, vermitteln jedoch Informationen, die unmittelbaren Einfluß auf unser Leben haben, wie etwa Verkehrsregeln oder Entfernungsangaben.* ■ *Les panneaux indiquant les lieux d'entreprises sont de plus en plus utilisés. De tels panneaux vont des styles primitifs, naïfs et amateurs jusqu'aux styles bien proportionnés, sophistiqués et térriblement passionnants. Parmi tous ces panneaux, les plus reconnaissables sont ceux qui montrent les logos et les marques des entreprises multinationales qui cherchent à répandre leur influence commerciale. Les signes routiers, quoiqu'ils soient omniprésents aussi, communiquent une information dont l'impact sur notre vie est plus immédiat, tels que les règlements des autoroutes ou la distance jusqu'à notre destination.*

Paris, France 1963

▲ **Marrakech,** Morocco 1975 ▶ **General store,** Oliverea, New York 1965 • **Gemischtwarenhandlung,** Olivera, New York 1965 • **Epicerie générale,** Oliverea, New York 1965

PEPSI say "Peps pleas

freshes ur. taste

Salem
refreshes your taste

Salem

Coca-Cola

7up

IS
So Good!

"fresh u with
7up

YTON

Pall Mall 100's
filters farther for a milder smoke

PALL MALL
MENTHOL

Puff for puff, milder than ever

Coca-Cola
12 oz.
Coca-Cola
12 oz.

WINSTON
tastes good

WINSTON
tastes good

KING SIZE
Winston
FULL RICH
TOBACCO FLAVOR

S
re
yo

S
FILTER C

So
Mild
So
Good

SUGAR FREE

DIET PEPSI

PRINGE
ALBERT
...the national joy sm
- SOLD HERE

Atlas Mountains, Morocco 1972

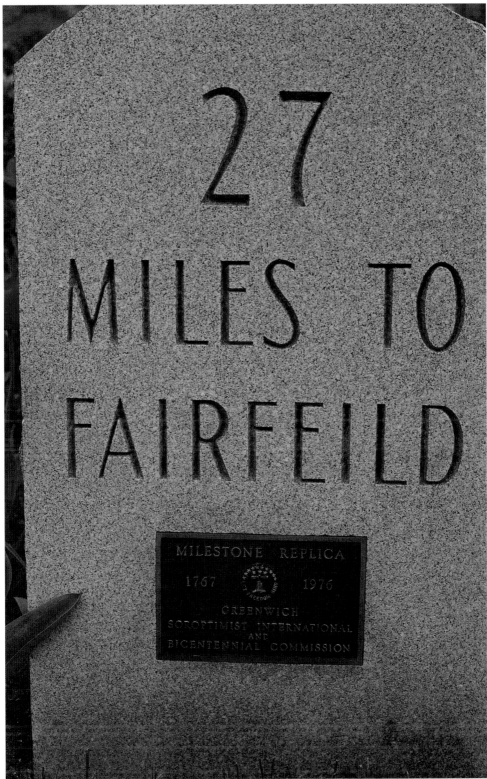

Milestone with misspelling, Greenwich, Connecticut 1985 • **Meilenstein mit falscher Schreibung,** Greenwich, Connecticut 1985 • **Borne kilométrique avec faute d'orthographe,** Greenwich, Connecticut 1985

House sign, Magdeburg, Germany 1971 • **Hausschild,** Magdeburg Deutschland 1971 • **Enseigne de maison à Magdeburg,** Allemagne 1971

Checkpoint Charlie, Berlin, Germany 1994

Berlin, Germany 1969

Berlin, Germany 1969

Marrakech, Morocco 1972

Victor, Colorado 1973

Home Office, British government, London, England 1965 • Britisches Innenministerium, London, England 1965 • Le "Home Office" du gouvernement britannique, Londres, Angleterre 1965

Street sign, Minneapolis, Minnesota 1978 • Straßenschild, Minneapolis, Minnesota 1978 • Enseigne des rue, Minnéapolis, Minnesota 1978

Pavement street sign, Charleston, South Carolina 1970 • Im Bürgersteig eingelassenes Straßenschild, Charleston, South Carolina 1970 • Enseigne des rues de Charleston, Caroline du Sud 1970

New Orleans, Louisiana 1972

Preservation Hall, New Orleans, Louisiana 1972

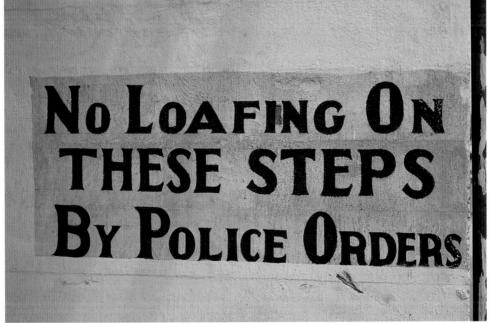

Front Royal, Virginia 1976

Bremen, Germany 1979

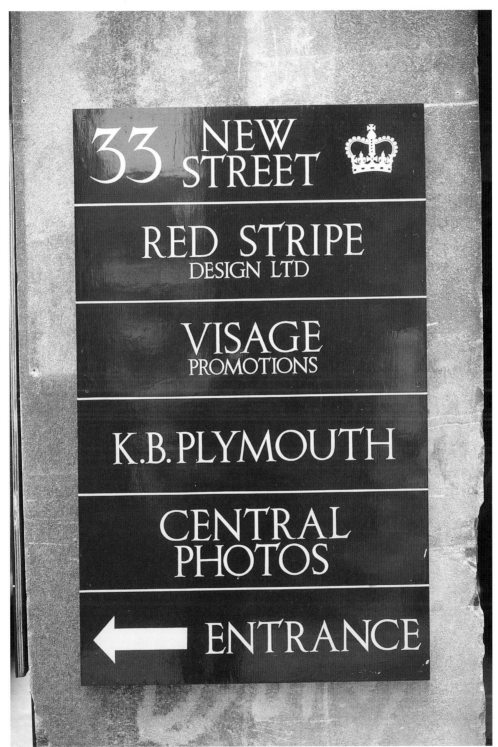

Plymouth, England 1985

London, England 1969

Portofino, Italy 1983

Paris, France 1969

North Tarrytown, New York 1970

Old New York state highway sign, North Tarrytown, New York 1970 • Altes Verkehrsschild des Staates New York, North Tarrytown, New York 1970 • Vieux signe routier, North Tarrytown, New York 1970

Old New York state highway sign, North Tarrytown, New York 1970 • Altes Verkehrsschild des Staates New York, North Tarrytown, New York 1970 • Vieux signe routier, North Tarrytown, New York 1970

San Juan, Puerto Rico 1988

London, England 1985

Old San Juan, Puerto Rico 1988

New Orleans, Louisiana 1973

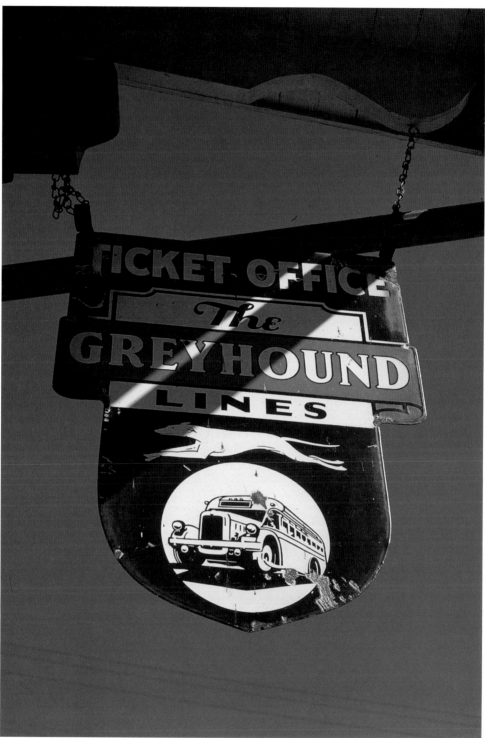

Orbisonia, Pennsylvania 1972

Jackson, New Hampshire 1971

Garrison, New York 1971

New Hope, Pennsylvania 1970

Whippany, New Jersey 1989

Arcade, New York 1987

Vintage steam tractor, Mount Pleasant, Iowa 1984 • **Alter Dampftraktor,** Mount Pleasant, Iowa 1984 • **Tracteur à vapeur d'époque,** Mount Pleasant, Iowa 1984

Speculator, New York 1969

Boston, Massachusetts 1968

Wolfeboro, New Hampshire 1982

Ringoes, New Jersey 1978

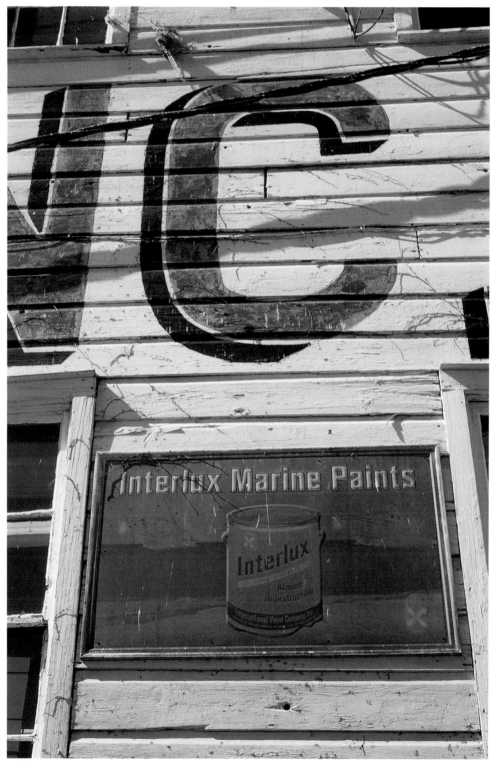

Upper Nyack, New York 1991

Baraboo, Wisconsin 1974

DRINKING
CONSULTANTS

Kelly's Korner

*arly signboards were generally painted or fashioned of wrought iron, particularly in Germanic countries. Typographically speaking, some of the most intriguing signs on hotels and inns date from the nineteenth and early twentieth centuries, while modern design makes abundant use of three-dimensional metal lettering and neon tubing. Similarly, theatre and cinema marquees, those oversized canopies of colored glass, metal, neon tubes, incandescent bulbs and frequently ill-spaced, movable block letters can enrapture or visually shock. ∎ Bars and pubs are among the oldest and most frequent establishments to announce their presence via signs. In earlier times, these signboards were almost invariably pictorial. Today these locales feature some of the most ornamented and typographically varied signs to be found. ∎ Frühe Firmenschilder wurden im allgemeinen gemalt oder aus Schmiedeeisen angefertigt, insbesondere in deutschsprachigen Ländern. Die aus typographischem Aspekt interessantesten Hotelschilder oder Gasthaustafeln stammen aus dem 19. und frühen 20. Jahrhundert; modernes Design macht reichlichen Gebrauch von dreidimensionalen Metallbuchstaben und Neonröhren. Ähnlich auch bei Theatern und Kinos: Überdimensionale Anzeigetafeln aus farbigem Glas, Metall, Neonlicht, Glühlampen und beweglichen Blockbuchstaben, oft mit unregelmässigen Abständen, können das Auge sowohl erfreuen als auch schockieren. ∎ Bars und Kneipen gehören zu den ältesten und häufigsten Einrichtungen, die durch Schilder auf sich aufmerksam machen. In früheren Zeiten bestanden diese Tafeln fast durchgängig aus bildlichen Darstellungen. Aber heute haben Bars und Pubs die meistverzierten und typographisch vielseitigsten Schilder. ∎ Les poteaux indicateurs étaient peints ou fabriqués en fer forgé, surtout dans des pays germaniques. Au niveau typographique, parmi les enseignes d'hôtels ou d'auberges les plus intéressantes, certaines datent du dix-neuvième siècle et du début du vingtième siècle; tandis qu'aujourd'hui le design utilise des caractères en métal à trois dimensions et des tuyaux au néon. De même, les marquises de théâtre et de cinéma, trop grandes et faites de verre coloré, de métal, de tuyaux au néon, d'ampoules incandescantes et de lettres interchangeables souvent mal espacées, peuvent enchanter ou choquer sur le plan visuel. ∎ Les bars et les pubs figurent parmi les établissements les plus vieux et les plus nombreux à annoncer leur présence à travers des enseignes. Au temps passé, ces enseignes étaient inévitablement picturales. Aujourd'hui, ces établissements de quartier sont équipés des enseignes les plus ornées et les plus variées sur le plan typographique qu'on puisse trouver.

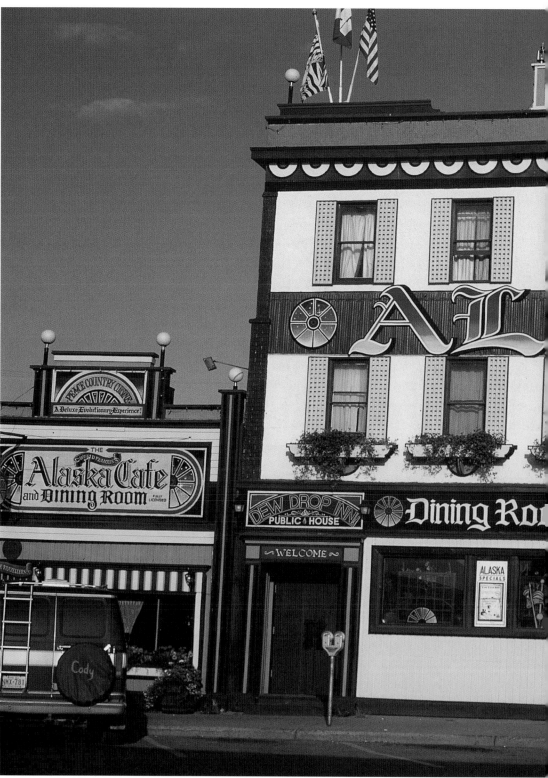

Dawson Creek, British Columbia, Canada 1993

Jim Thorpe, Pennsylvania 1988

Killarney, Ireland, 1995

Cochem, Germany 1972

Bed & Breakfast, Südheiderstedt, Holstein, Germany 1990 • **Fremdenzimmer-Pension,** Südheiderstedt, Holstein, Deutschland 1990 • **Un hôtel bed and breakfast,** Südheiderstedt, Holstein, Allemagne 1990

Wichita, Kansas, 1994

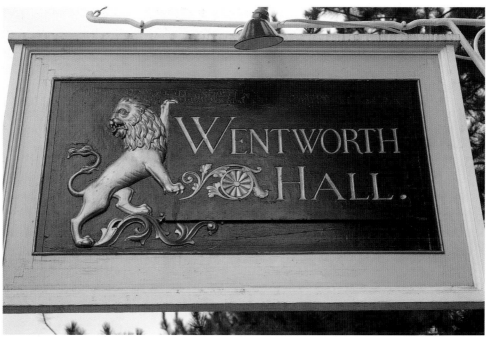

Jackson, New Hampshire 1971

Chicago, Illinois 1984

Durbin, West Virginia 1980

Cripple Creek, Colorado 1973

Old Sacramento, California 1988

Sturbridge, Massachusetts 1968

Wells, England 1985

Hattenheim, Germany 1975

Inverness, Scotland 1985

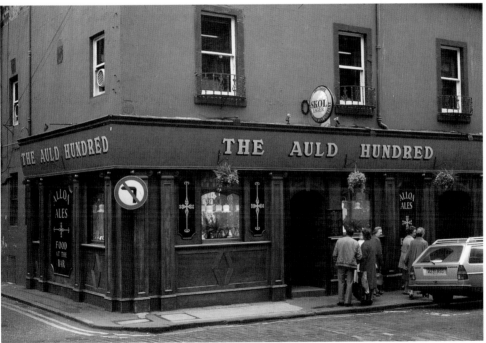

Edinburgh, Scotland 1985

FINE FOODS & SPIRITS
GALLAGHER'S
AT WHARFSIDE
LICENSED PREMISES

◄ **Victoria,** British Columbia, Canada 1981 ▲ **Aspen,** Colorado 1984

Las Vegas, Nevada 1973

Windsor, England 1985

London, England 1985

Windsor, England 1985

Zürich, Switzerland 1970

Rüdesheim, Germany 1980

Frankfurt am Main, Germany 1969

Chester, England 1985

Hammersmith, London, England 1985

Paris, France 1969

Brigham City, Utah 1976

Tokyo, Japan 1989

Toronto, Ontario Canada 1993

Canaan, Connecticut 1994

Cripple Creek, Colorado 1973

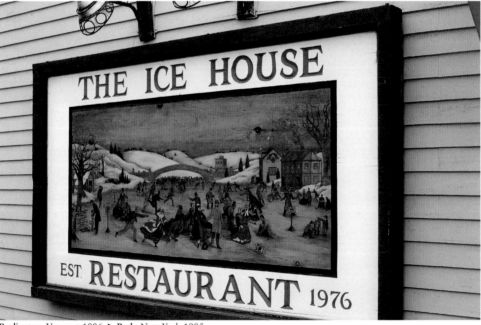

Burlington, Vermont 1986 ▶ **Bath,** New York 1985

Montreal, Quebec, Canada 1974

City of Quebec, Quebec, Canada 1977

Indianapolis, Indiana 1992

Traverse City, Michigan 1993

◄Chicago, Illinois 1984 ▲ Chicago, Illinois 1992

The Tappan Zee Playhouse, Nyack, New York 1973

In our time-obsessed, fast-moving society with its digital time displays measuring even tenths of seconds, it is a reassuring and calming pleasure to rest our eyes upon a twelve-hour clock surface with legible Arabic or stately Roman numerals and beautifully ornamented, or simple and functional hands. ■ When one is of the mind to reflect on the past or to explore the typographic fashions of yesteryear, the chiseled inscriptions of ancient tombstones propel us into our collective memory. ■ In unserer zeitbesessenen, schnellebigen Gesellschaft mit ihren sogar Zehntelsekunden messenden digitalen Zeitanzeigen ist es wohltuend und beruhigend, den Blick ruhen zu lassen auf einem 12-Stunden-Ziffernblatt mit lesbaren arabischen oder vornehmen römischen Zahlen und mit verschnörkelten oder einfachen und funktionalen Uhrzeigern. ■ Wenn einem der Sinn danach steht, über die Vergangenheit nachzudenken oder die typographischen Gepflogenheiten von gestern zu erforschen, dann führen uns die feingemeißelten Inschriften alter Grabsteine in unser kollektives Gedächtnis. ■ Dans notre société trop obsédée par le temps, en mouvement constant, brandissant ces chronomètres mesurant même le dixième d'une seconde, il est rassurant et calmant de pouvoir fixer nos yeux sur la surface d'une horloge aux chiffres arabes ou romains, lisibles et joliment ornés ou aux aiguilles simples et fonctionnelles. ■ Quand on est disposé à réfléchir au passé ou à explorer les styles typographiques en vogued'antan, les inscriptions ciselées sur les pierres tombales anciennes nous renvoient à notre mémoire collective.

North Tarrytown, New York 1968

Bladen, England 1985

Carmel Mission, California 1991

New Orleans, Louisiana 1976

Dessau, Germany 1971

Rabat, Morocco 1972

Salzburg, Austria 1979

Chicago, Illinois 1987

Nördlingen, Germany 1970

Chicago, Illinois 1987

Traverse City, Michigan 1993

Waterbury, Connecticut 1993

Chicago, Illinois 1987

Berlin, Germany 1969

Heide, Germany 1991

Chester, England 1985

Crates for the Soviet Union, Dessau, East Germany 1971 • **Kisten für die Sowjetunion,** Dessau, DDR 1971 • **Les caisses à destination de l'Union Soviétique,** Dessau, Allemagne de l'Est 1971

Store in Frankfurt am Main, Germany 1972 • **Geschäft in Frankfurt am Main,** Deutschland 1972 • **Magasin à Frankfurt am Main,** Allemagne 1972